THINGS I MUST HAVE KNOWN

THINGS I MUST HAVE KNOWN

POETRY

A. B. SPELLMAN

COFFEE HOUSE PRESS
MINNEAPOLIS
2008

COFFEE HOUSE PRESS books are available to the trade through our primary distributor, Consortium Book Sales & Distribution, www.cbsd.com or (800) 283-3572. For personal orders, catalogs, or other information, write to: Coffee House Press, 27 North Fourth Street, Suite 400, Minneapolis, MN 55401.

Coffee House Press is a nonprofit literary publishing house. Support from private foundations, corporate giving programs, government programs, and generous individuals helps make the publication of our books possible. We gratefully acknowledge their support in detail in the back of this book.

To you and our many readers around the world, we send our thanks for your continuing support.

LIBRARY OF CONGRESS CIP INFORMATION
Spellman, A.B., 1935–
Things I must have known : poems / by A.B. Spellman.
p. cm.
ISBN-13: 978-1-56689-211-7
ISBN-10: 1-56689-206-6
1. Title.
PS3569.P444T47 2008
811'.54—DC22
2007046531

FIRST EDITION | FIRST PRINTING
1 3 5 7 9 8 6 4 2

ACKNOWLEDGMENTS
"Song Of The Luddite" appeared in *Massachusetts Review;* "The Truth About Karen" and "After Vallejo" in *African American Review,* and "Hellfighters On Parade" in *Poet Lore.*

FOR KAREN

CONTENTS

11 After Vallejo

13 Dear John Coltrane

15 Why Do They Call It Nightmare When a Horse Is What You Need?

17 Groovin' Low

18 Astrology

20 Ghost

23 Observers Are Worried. Believers Are Enjoying

31 Out of Nazareth

35 Hellfighters on Parade

37 Sojourner's Song

39 Metrarie

41 Colleague

42 Cloud, as You

44 When Black People Are

46 Another Love Song

51 The City Poet on the Stroll

56 The Call

58 Pearl

61 Pearl 2

65 The Truth about Karen

67 Thursday, Early April

68 Toyin's Sound

72 Oriki

73 The Meeting

75 Song of the Luddite

77 Random Memory

79 Time Was

81 The Unrequited Lust Blues

82 On Hearing Gonzalo Rubalcaba at Blues Alley

85 On Hearing Sonny ("Newk") Rollins in the Park on a
    Hot Summer Night

87 Bobby's Ballad

89 Notes on a Poem: Summer (Verano); César Vallejo

90 The View Behind

92 Theology

97 October

99 9/11/01

101 The Cruelest Month

102 How Freedom Works for Small Things

103 Villanelle for the Hell of It

104 Things I Miss From My Youth

113 Things I Don't Miss From My Youth

120 Redemption Song

122 The First Seventy

131 Wrong Again

133 Origins

136 In Which I Slam the Wilson

137 Death Poem

141 Conclusion

144 Notes

AFTER VALLEJO

i will die in havana in a hurricane
it will be morning, i'll be facing southwest
away from the gulf, away from the storm
away from home, looking to the virid hills
of matanzas where the orisha rise, lifted
by congueros in masks of iron, bongoseros
in masks of water, timbaleros in masks of fire
by all the clave that binds the rhythms of this world

i'll be writing when i go, revising another
hopeful survey of my life. i will die of nothing
that i did but of all that i did not do
i promised myself a better self
than i could make & i will not forgive

you will be there, complaining
that i never saved you, that i left you
where you live, stranded
in your own green dream

when you come for me come singing
no dirge, but scat my eulogy in bebop
code. sing that i died among gods
but lived with no god & did not suffer
for it. find one true poem that i made

& sing it to my shade as it fades
into the wind. sing it presto, in 4/4 time
in the universal ghetto key of b flat

i will die in havana in rhythm. tumbao
montuno, guaguanco, dense strata
of rhythm pulsing me away
                              & the mother of waters
will say to the saint of crossroads
well, damn. he danced his way out after all

DEAR JOHN COLTRANE

—with acknowledgments to Michael Harper

dead night has me writing poetry

in another hotel room. j.s. bach

is on the radio. the keyboard concerto

in f minor: the one you also hear

on oboe or violin. the largo

second movement begins

& the book in my hand drops

the room fades

& i put my reason down

to trail the bach of endless line

along this earthless path, each note full

& bright, a brilliant footprint on the dark

through beauty, past knowledge, into

that state that shines too much

to be wisdom, is too transparent

to be art. i catch a fear of the place

where he will lower me when

this transporting melody closes

then it closes on itself & here i am

dear john, back at the beginning, better

later, different station, cold room dimming

it's you, john, *trane's slow blues*

now it's your line that opens, & opens
& opens, & i'm flying that way again
same sky, different moon, this midnight
globe that toned those now lost blue rooms
where things like jazz float the mind
this motion the still & airless propulsion
i know as inner flight. this view
the one i cannot see with my eyes
open. i hear the beginning approach, &
i know the line i traveled was a horizon
the circle of the world. another freedom
flight to another starting place

if i believed in heaven i would ask
if you & bach ever swap infinite fours
& jam the sound that light makes
going & coming, & if you exchange maps
to those exclusive clouds you travel thru
& do you give them names?

WHY DO THEY CALL IT NIGHTMARE WHEN A HORSE IS WHAT YOU NEED?

i hate it, this dream
where the thing of indeterminate mass
gimlet eyes drilling the back of my head
breath that bears the heat
of hell is after me & i'm running hard
trying to put a few skyscrapers between me
& it on my way out of town
i'm thinking: i've got plenty of time
this prowling theriomorph is slow
though it's ugly as pain
but my goddamn feet take me nowhere
& the street that looks solid enough
becomes this treadmill that rolls under me
& shit! the big fuzzy lump is gaining

you've probably dreamt this too. your beast
closing, your laboring legs failing. maybe
you've looked it up, even consulted someone
who collects garbage dreams & it's all cogent
text to you. you know where this hirsute figment
sleeps when you don't, which parts of your jiva
it feeds on, its never-spoken name. myself

i don't want to be too intimate with vague demons
that chase me in screaming impotence
toward a death that isn't there
i just want my feet to work

GROOVIN' LOW

my swing is more mellow
these days: not the hardbop drive
i used to roll but more of a cool
foxtrot. my eyes still close
when the rhythm locks; i've learned
to boogie with my feet on the floor
i'm still movin', still groovin'
still fallin' in love

i bop to the bass line now. the trap set
paradiddles ratamacues & flams
that used to spin me in place still set me
off, but i bop to the bass line now
i enter the tune from the bottom up
& let trumpet & sax wheel above me

so don't look for me in the treble
don't look for me in the fly
staccato splatter of the hot young horn
no, you'll find me in the nuance
hanging out in inflection & slur
i'm the one executing the half-bent
dip in the slow slowdrag
with the smug little smile
& the really cool shades

ASTROLOGY

just back from eternity she applies
to the indifferent bijouterie
of the upper night for the comfort
no hand has given her. would she accept
a hand? she thinks she would
but never has. hand, sky
any consummate deed thing or being
to confirm her sapience beyond the paltry fact
that she was here to ask the question
"is there perhaps some worse state
than alive?" not quite ready to settle
for so bare a living she asks the stars again
is certain that they answered
is uncertain what they said

the weight of all this nothing
the imminent prospect of unbecoming
has made a harlequin of her
on the chance that she might catch
her painted grin laughing back
in a passing window & crack up
at such silly profile, that laughter
lust or some other art would seep down
to that deep cellar where the good wine's
stored & libate these blues away

o stars o moon o runes of night
o spirit wine o blues
know something! know something! know!

but what of the proximate night
whose amative intimacies the body holds?
lovers, friends, home, that kind of theater
still playing on this side of shadow
they have light with them too
but no! those mysteries are solved
& do not answer now
they are too much the life
the life too much the cause

to stare out of the self
into this picayune globe of feckless trust
she throws her eye into the speckled dark
& stacks its minute revelations
one by one in hope that they'd compose
into useful discovery &
scans the cosmic lines in hope
of parsing this untransposed vacuity
with what she thinks to be
the cold distant wisdom
on the roof of night, the cryptic script
of the only god she can see

GHOST

she had lost him
in the most exasperating way
a stupid hiking accident
not even a story worth the telling
& he was gone, replaced
by this cold & empty not-him
waxen figure posed before her
in the perverse absurdity of death

they had loved so long
the best of her had nowhere else
to go. her struts & beams
were dismantled & carted away
& the little she had left could not stand
against a vagrant breeze
which made his peculiar presence-
in-absence so hard to grip
he seemed to wander
the far corners of her periphery
there he was at the edge of sight
buying italian ice from the man
with the yellow cart—no he was
that gentleman who looked so lost
in midtown as he always was . . .

the hermeneutic arguments
they'd always had they still held
& still he won as many as he lost
though now she spoke to him
without the slightest dissembling
in the unmannered tones we reserve
for the intimate dead

spirit. she called him that: spirit
her faith held spirit to be outside of time
& space, for all dimensions failed
in a state where his spirit walked
beside & inside her while her own
suddenly friable soul disintegrated
into sparkling atoms
of nothing. time was no more
than a sequence of foggy windows
which vaguely framed his image

                          absence
does that to a love
it shifted the landmarks
of her life so she couldn't chart
where she was or where she'd been
the reliquaries of their years together
no longer pertained—the photographs
the letters back & forth would be profound
souvenirs someday but now were statements
without tense or gender

but wasn't that him . . .

so she stationed him between dream
& cognition so that all the light that left her
all the light that entered her
bent through him & hazed her days
with welcome memories. the quarrels
the rude scents, the irritating habits
purged from her recollection. she knew
she must conceal this new-made sanity
or be thought insane. trusting heaven
she did not distinguish what the mind makes
from what is made for the singular mind

having called his spirit in
she held it close. accepted
that when the giver takes
he leaves a part behind. she made a home
for him in the place her heart had been
& was glad he loved enough to remain

OBSERVERS ARE WORRIED. BELIEVERS ARE ENJOYING

—sign on a cab somewhere in africa

in the masque
of cities
the old man speaks

unto

maker of makers
made herself
near where
earth now floats
which was cool
until the great empty
divided into yes
& no
which wasn't

unto was favored
with intelligence
which let her
do
but cursed with
imagination
which made

her lonesome
lonesome hurts
even a maker

was it
because unto was
so small
smaller than this
or even that?
we cannot guess
not even
the most learned
for she never said
& speculation
would trap us
in the makers'
game

so our being
is our burden
for we are made
of the soft
stuff
of fantasy &
makers
like the rest
of us dream
crooked

                                  unto loved threes
                    you've heard
                    of the kiss
                    of life but
                    there were
                    three. she
                    kissed us
                    between the eyes
                    above the left
                    nipple &
                    on that tender place
                    at the nape
                    of the crotch

& here came
that awful life
lust cause
after
unto made one
she made
another
& then a third &
left it to
the three to finish
thinking three
a full number
o.k. from a god's
point of view

but the three
was us
& you *know*
we fucked that up

          we went straight
          to yes
          (man
          in horny excess)
          & no (woman
          in self defense)
          & well . . .
          (man / woman / man
          being cool) &
          that's how
          procreation
          originated war

poor unto had everything
of the world
to make so
naturally she made
more makers:
first she made
hardmaker
who was to give
everybody someplace

to walk
ocean beds, dirt
mountains, etc.

flowmaker who
put process
in the world
with air, water
blood, slobber
flatulent wind
tears too
which were flo's
proudest
invention because
tears made
a substance
of feeling

unto was smart
she knew a world
would need
action
so she made
consumption
who then made
death who gave
birth a place
to start. but birth

was too weak
to make
by herself
i mean birth
of from with
whom?
                    so birth
asked unto
for a trigger
& unto gave her
conception
the thought thing
who was impotent
without a body
to drive
which circles us
back to the war
of the three

you see
the problem here?
unto made us
& her makers but
she never thought to
introduce anybody
& everything
had to find
everybody & it
was all a mess

nobody ever decided
who anybody
belonged to
so air allies
with fire but fights
water
which fights
earth. worse
birth
& death became
conflicts not
resolutions

well, you & i
are human we
have to account
for the goofs
of the gods
who fail cause
making is such
detail work
they never see
the panorama
you think unto
clapped her hands
& bang!
the universe?

no sir no
ma'am. she stitched
this joint together
mote to
bloody mote
so makers think
so teeny
they leave
the big death
eternity questions
to us who
are too scared
to think them thru

that's why we grew fear
& worry
poor sustenance
but whatchu
gonna do?

OUT OF NAZARETH

pilate the procurator, mean bastard that he was
thought three hours a mercifully quick death
for this, what's his name? jew. he, pilate
was satisfied that he'd played the rabble well

the soldiers thought it a routine dispatch
for a slave or one not graced to be born roman

tired of holier-than-thou ascetics
in a town where prophets pitched gnosis
on every corner, the sadducee rabbis were smug
they dared him to miracle his broke ass
out of this one

his buddies lay low as he said they would

if the distant patriarch he called on
in the only prayer he ever taught noticed
his response was skimpy: black sky, small tremor
cracked rocks, a few crypt doors popped open
nothing major, nothing grand

manual for crucifixion: you prepare the apostate
by flogging. have him carry the crossbeam through the streets
to where the stake is securely planted. a crowd
always turns out for a lynching & they will taunt him
with insults & throw refuse. let them. it makes a good show
keeps the people happy & gives the prisoner the full benefit
of the experience by letting him die humiliated. attach his feet
one atop the other to a little plank of olive wood
with a single spike & drive that into the stake. do *not*
nail the hands to the crossbeam—they will break free &
then you've got a mess. instead affix the forearms
to it. a board under the hips will hold the body up
& better excruciate the miscreant. he'll eventually die
of suffocation & if you do it right the demise
will take days. to check for the imminence of death
look for bottomless thirst, then awful shudders
of course, you could be nice & break his legs
or ribs so the shock releases him faster. *always*
stab him in the heart to make sure that he's dead
so he doesn't get buried alive. no need to be cruel

3

the marys came for him loaded with perfumes
to defend against the awful reek
of deadtown. instead they walked into a light
in the gloaming, a speaking light in the room
of the dead. speaking light that threw no shadows

in a voice that made no sound. he's not here
the light said you won't find him in deadtown
the terrible voice in the glow said to the marys
in this putrescent place of the missing dead
words in the glow of the life of the dead
shook the marys to the quick. the men
thought them hysterical

4

paul, jew of tarsus, snitch for the pharisees
fresh from the lapidation of stephen
met jesus from the foot of his horse
in a coma, blind from the light, the word
of the way in his ear, paul fell into the faith
he would make from scratch & take
to the uncircumcised of flesh & uncircumcised
of heart & out of the uptight law of moses

now off to fight the bloody bull of mithras
sweet isis, daughter of earth & sky
cybele, great succulent mother of us all
writing letters to the faithful as he went

5

celsus, pagan & proud of it, thought he'd look
into this new galilean custom: the unanimity
was impressive, & you hadda give them the morality
which was hard to come by in rome. & man

33

could they blow. but face it, their audience
was children & silly women, especially widows
especially widows with money, & their eloquence
was the eloquence of frogs
but who could take seriously their dictum
that the cosmos with all of its back & forth
lived in each of us. rome had it right. better
to take the gods of all nations into battle
with them. especially the ones more manly than this

HELLFIGHTERS ON PARADE

so there's the 15th heavyfoot regiment band
the harlem hellfighters, james reese europe
director, tuning up. they got a french horn
choir & enough trumpets & t'bones to call down
the saints. hell, they got marimbaphones &
double b-flat helicons; they got all the brass
you can mass on the grass. they got bill robinson
for drum major so you know they can kick
& they're looking good: knickers creased
to the side & tight wrapped leggings
boots got more sparkle than glass
croix de guerre ribbons puff their chests

they form. on europe's cue they rag *How
Ya Gonna Keep 'Em Down On The Farm
After They've Seen Paree* in a shim sham shimmy
kinda march that j.p. sousa never heard of
the hellfighters blow their way up fifth avenue
& the ticker tape snows down &
the white folks' cheers lift the clouds

you'd've thought to see it that america'd changed

but proud picture postcards from dixie
still hit new york of "nigger barbecues"
autos-da-fé of black heroes back from the war

ruined by the taste of honor, who walked as
the hellfighters walk, too proud to live, staked
& burning, their complaining wives & sisters too
before those awful deadpanned faces
slow cameras caught. "close the school jeb
the kids need to see this. they're running
an extra train from atlanta so i'll make sandwiches
& lemonade to sell to the tourists &
for god's sake pick up the trash. we want
the town to look good for all the dignitaries"

so on the march uptown europe broods
through the throb of his fiery corns
just whose hell did we fight anyway?

but now at lenox avenue in sweet harlem
the music hits the sidewalk & explodes
bold & living, tangible, its own force in the world
it springs the heels of fine brown ladies
who pump the mana into the sound, the hot afflatus
of the rising home. 'jangles, legs no longer weary
strutting like a guinea fowl in estrus, his kick
gone higher in a cakewalk with the sisters
& spatted swells flush with the pride of renewal
the mighty doughboys are again the darktown
strutters. call the tune, professor europe

"well, hit it boys: *Here Comes Your Daddy Now*
sweet mama, *Here Comes Your Daddy Now*"

SOJOURNER'S SONG

If a man have a quart and a woman a pint,
why can't her little pint be full?
—ISABELLA VAN WAGENEN, a.k.a. SOJOURNER TRUTH

"suck on these," sojourner truth
 told the slavists who heckled her
"your children have" & bared her breasts,
 now long & limp, a wilted field
 of black against the vestal
 linen she always wore

 they'd accused her of being a man. had
 to be. no pertness to her. none of the belleishness
 about her that said "woman"
 sojourner's belly-rumbled voice
 a low brass wind that hit them in their arrogance
 & brought them low, these supercilious men
 so smug they'd make a slave of man woman
 or child, a critter to be worked fed
 beaten or fucked according to their needs

 had to be a man. proper women
 even white ones, did not stand & speak
 to men this way, did not make little joshuas
 of themselves & trumpet at the walls

of fortress south. & when they said
they'd burn down the hall she roared
"then i'll speak upon the ashes." speak
upon the ashes! see her stand tall
all black in white above the mound
of soot beneath her, arms spread
wide in the image of the god
she'd made for herself, loving god
of the vision & the silent voice
that named her sojourner truth

who in our time does this work? the smolder
of our pride lays ash everywhere. but who
creates what god they need to step beyond
their sex &, naked, stand above the cinders
to call the power down? those bombastic men
like ours had their god & scripture
like ours made war beneath his name
like ours they stained the night with blood
& orchestrated days with cannon fire
so they could govern earth & all the wealth
it spouts. who now wields the clarion to bring
them low? who tells them "suck on these?"

METRARIE

—L.A., Circa 1860

in the hub of the night
blank spot in the bayou
under moon round & fertile
freemen, freedmen, slave, free
in the dark, bare to the skin
bare in the skin, blacker than dark
fair as the moon, 'round an altar
of stumps upon ground soaked
to the bone of the earth
with blood of pullet, blood of hog
dance the faithful with offerings
of rum, poundcake, pieces of home

houngan & mambo, drums
of all nations, dance calinda
congo pile, call loa down
papa legba old & thin, he smokes
too much. baron samedi conducts
the dead, may he leave home
his hateful guede with all the conflict
of hell upon them. damballa snakes
the belly to the ground
                              & the loa ride

39

voodoo, voodooienne, veves in the dust
articulate the dance

'

all know to be taken, be danced
from the spirit out, tell what
the loa tell in voices they cannot hear
they speak in the glossolalia of serpents
from a puissance
that is stronger than chains.
loose the spirit
from flesh in the hub of the dark

tomorrow returns more brutal than night

houngan & mambo know no dance against it

COLLEAGUE

refuse this cold scripture of the commonplace
at your risk, tight little man. you gotta turn & turn
& turn again from those dismal arrivals
your nature insists upon & lighten up. this foaming
fake ebullience that you advertise doesn't sell &
you need a new hook. how in hell & with what material
did you make this clever, polished, buttoned down
ruin that you are? with aspects of a working premise
now long forgotten because it failed when it was new?
probably that hagiographic statue you daydream
of commissioning of yourself requires this pose
of you, nostrils flared up to the rain
the feral conniving eyes that peek out of you
pretending a jovial wisdom, volumes you've neither written
nor read cupped in your hand. you credit yourself
as some short gnomon whose shadow describes
the whole earth's rotation

well your shadow is just an absence of light
little man. know this & stand in the dark

CLOUD, AS YOU

from the perspective of the cottonball cloud
that coasts above you in apparent serenity
the crooked red lightning that cracks out of it
to split the sky is not necessarily
an antonym of peace

unlike the dormant you who
makes unwelcome speeches to yourself
in that annoying retrolingual voice
from beneath all those layers
of mad choices made & deferred
that comprise you, commanding
that you stretch at last
beyond yourself, deep into
the esoteric dimension of the living
& find someplace to rest
a foot, polite conversation
with someone unlike you
some tangible item of comfort
to wear against your skin

you cark your nerves with a panic
analogous to the voltage
the cloud imparts that your ease
in estrangement will be compromised
if you evacuate this amniotic emptiness

this is how waking feels
when you sleep without dreams
a tense stasis, neither day
nor night, retreat nor advance
despite that goddamn bugle
the world blows in your ear. fall
back / spring forward
you eclipse your own light

from the perspective of the lightning
out of the belly of the seemingly
innocent cloud, you there spinning
in the vortex between thinking &
feeling & living numb are a thing
to break. it sees neither the in
nor the out of you
it only strikes

WHEN BLACK PEOPLE ARE

when black people are
with each other
we sometimes fear ourselves
whisper over our shoulders
about unmentionable acts
& sometimes we fight & lie
these are some things we sometimes do

& when alone i sometimes walk
from wall to wall fighting visions
of white men fighting me
& black men fighting white men
& fighting me & i lose my
self between walls &
ricocheting shots & can't say
for certain who i have killed
or been killed by

.it is the fear of winter passing
& summer coming & the killing
i have called for coming
to my door saying
hit it a.b., you're in it too

& the white army moves like thieves
in the night mass-producing beautiful
black corpses & then stealing them away
while my frequent death watches me
from orangeburg on cronkite &
i'm oiling my gun & cooking my food
& saying "when the time comes"
to myself, over & over, hopefully

but i remember driving from atlanta
to birmingham with stone & featherstone
& cleve & feather talked
about dueling a pair of klansmen
& cleve told how they hunted chaney's
schwerner's & goodman's bodies
in the haunted hours of the silver nights
in the mississippi swamp while a runaway survivor
from orangeburg slept between wars
on the back seat

times like this
are times when black people
are with each other & the strength flows
back & forth between us like
borrowed breath

—1968

ANOTHER LOVE SONG

dread is the hook & it hooks into us & the walk
among our brothers twists the thing
makes an attitude of nearness that never lets us truly laugh
or truly love or truly rest
at peace. it is a subtle distress, this fear that we are the hook
of our brothers: that they know
the good things we are not, the foul things that we are,
hook so deeply caught the brothers hurt
inside us, all fetus-bent & pointed to the heart
the rhyme they rap is the pain that breaks our voice
it shouts from our center, shouts from the face
reflected in the spilled blood at the foot of the stoop
we are the brothers, fear us

on the corners the brothers strut their dread
before the electric glass where the gold of the age
brays its concupiscent might. this lush dread sports
golden hair that mimes the sun
wears a thong & drives a slick car. this whore
eidolon fucks us dry & claims we'll never die
of its fatal sensuality. love this dread & know the hook
of the pipe & the spike

our america, an upas tree we camp below, drips
its milk of dread upon us, waves a star-spangled
dread in the lie of justice. it offers just enough to tease

the brothers: see? we bust no more
than a third of you, kill but the déclassé among you
the rest, you fair & schooled ones, are free
to crawl the length of your leashes on your carpets
& hardwoods, in your beamers & silks

the brothers lovingly dread america as she lies
laughing, naked, behind the glowing glass, gives
the hook a post-coital twist from her perch on our rods
for what can be more freak than to cum
to your murder? how can she not laugh in her slow
drag to our soul's vitiation, fondling
her bikini bones through the living glass? she laughs
when the brothers thank her for the dance
thank her for the fuck through the crystal condom
thank her for our death, & name it just

the brothers did, yes, bring the music to the party, did
teach the hip-hop moves to the bone dancer
did write the lyric to the backbeat lust, did name the sisters
mere meat for the bone. their reduction
is the love song to the golden-haired thong thing
that shimmies behind the electric glass. such lust
hones the hook in the heart, fills the spike, lights the pipe
(here a press roll to the bump & grind)

& the sisters dread the brothers' bone lust popping
on the streets. it is procreant but hates a home
the sisters love love, the slow walk through the years

the near warm spot beneath the covers

every single night, the whispered yes that confirms tomorrow

true deep humming love of the sisters is the dread hook

answer. the hook fills the heartspace where

the sister ought to rest. she will circle in

if we clear a place for her. say yes to the dance

toward forever with the strong brown woman

remember:

they sent us moses. but which moses did they send?

not the militant thaumaturge who blasted locusts

fire & death at egypt till the chains broke, not

the moses of the long march, the hand

of the yahweh who drowned horse & rider

the mouth of yahweh, lord of the beaten & torn

see him with his arms raised roiling the sea, looking

like john brown, the son of thunder

the terrible moses we needed but had to make

ourselves only to see them kill him as malcolm

& again as martin. no, they gave us moses lawbringer

him of the burning bush & the rules

for us alone. moses with the god voice

commanding "yield." unbending moses

of the staff who would discipline our souls &

they sent us jesus. (bereft of faith i do not clasp

his intervening invisible cosmic hand. have

no sight through the metaphysical eye or dream

of unending life past life. but if the enduring voice

of jesus calls the brothers to the act of holding

'gainst the crush of empty gain, i will honor it)

but what jesus did they call? not the sharp

nappy-haired semitic jew who threw the shekels

in the street & chased the usurers from the temple stoop

they sent gnostic yeshua, abstract moralist

whose mission was cool with the way things were

this blond swedish looking theocentrist

with the plaintive eyes bent up & out of this world

who taught it would all get better when you die

not the militant ascetic whose primacy of the

poor the sadducees thought seditious—no

they sent us gethsemane jesu, lord of the knees

whose yoke was easy & whose burden was light

not the cristos of jeremiah who fed the poor &

hated the rich but the jesu of aquinas

who hovered out of reach of culture & beamed

rays of glory down on us. matthean jesu

who fed the poverty of the spirit & let the belly bloat

who preached that meekness in this life

would earn us milk & honey

in the gold-paved streets of heaven forever

such afreets devil the brothers in the dread
intersection of eternal & diurnal where the bone lust
breeds. we ply the power that beats us down
upon the sisters when no dick is scepter enough
to proclaim a brother pharaoh. the brothers fly
to the cross face-first where our spent flesh awaits
the feast of the dread bone ghost

& dread is the hook & it hooks into us

THE CITY POET ON THE STROLL

—for Gaston Neal

my fast walking buddy slowed down
for forever he's spun 'round corners
his hustle in his bag, his habit in overdrive
too quick for the breeze; too slick for the roller

14th & u changed colors in the streaking seasons
before & after us. jelly roll, hustler to the bone
the lordly duke, swooped through here, derbied
& spatted, wolfing on soft-hatted women
all fine in their honeyed aspect

walls of his heart, cool blow that whips
the flame, the corner's dancing gravitons
pull the brown swells home
my buddy's base spot in pittsburgh
the crawford grill, housed bebop liberated
hip boys swung out of cab's neat seats
with reet pleats into yardbird's redefined tweeds
& shades. my hip talking buddy
told stories of the pittsburgh hill: murphy men
playing on the respectable greedy. knife fights
in the pool room that didn't even stop the games
my buddy danced them to life for white
the mad painter, & me

in our new day, '56-'57, 9th & u, 14th & u
sweet & sour georgia avenue, were as swinging
as d.c. owned. some flicks in this block
latin dance in that loft, hardbop in this basement
brown bags in that cabaret, fats domino
& pegleg bates at the howard. i knew
the facades & parlors; my quick stepping
buddy knew the back rooms & alleys
upstairs at abarts buck & gus & stump let me sing on the last set

to a near empty room; i like to think because the squares
had split & they thought the crowd down enough
but in truth they were tired so here, a.b., have the mike
angel eyes in c. i wanted a cool like johnny hartman's
my next buddy didn't care. he wanted to rap about the mallarmé
in my back pocket. i knew books but craved the corners
city poets from baudelaire to langston had told me of
he knew the streets but craved the books he had no guide for

he said

so go there with me. i know hard nuance
that will decorate the rills of your brain
with glow & shadow. rooms of this limp city
where men still jam the delta blues in time
to the rimshot percussion of dice against the baseboard
know back doors to alleys where the trade
is in pleasures of the edge of the skin. the senses
order rules: you learn to see as the blind see

with the light of knowing what the books
don't teach. with the omniscient eye
of living when the power wants you dead

　　　yes, i said

come here with me. i know verse
that will not leave you even as the years
abbreviate memory. lines to make a family
of. show you that thought you almost had
when the gray sickness enclosed you &
the scream wouldn't sound. how like the streets
the broken-line page is: you read it down
below your reason, down beneath the bottom
where mad lost truth cringes & hides

　　　　　* * *

but the streets are treacherous in their virtue
scag poisoned my swift stepping buddy, put
a dip in his stance & a slide in his stride. snaked
a new set of veins all through him. tracked a map
of scars 'round his now tilting form. scag
whored his love of books. bent the eye
the radical of his poems, down to corrupted
concrete earth. still my book-hustling buddy
made a lyric of the stroll, sang poems of walls
made of roaches near the '64 14th & u
where the demon dooji hung

53

no blood-humping parasite could eat my buddy
whole. i saw him build a school of pan-african
dreams where the art of struggle crossed
the bloody waters from home to home: black
flame of the burning streets, flame of the muted
poor, flame of his flaming corner. he danced
through the crumbling walls with mad men &
mad dogs, screaming, kill martin? kill malcolm?
      kill me

      we are not the only people who celebrate the death
      of our heroes by dying; are not alone in our festival
      of bones; do not sing solo before the tumescent flame
      we pantomime war in our dance of release & ululate
      "fire" in chorus at the brilliant air till it burns our throats
      & call it victory. we are alone in this collective isolation
      this black isthmus where i eats i & america, jailer & father
      gives us the material to construct heroes better than cities

from that time he hears the near teutonic music
of jackboots breaking the air as they descend
toward his face. no fault there. it is the nature
of jackboot wearers to abhor the cries of those
whom they have caused to hurt, to crave silence
from the voice-warriors of the burning night

no fault here. my heart-first buddy hooked
the corners the alleys the readers & rappers

to the fire & sirens. brought the brown classes
to the venue of the city poem where dawn
is closure for the after-hours hustler, the moon
a lamp to work by, faith is the next vein shot
& hope is the will not to die today

my flipped-out buddy knows such madness
has value. out too far, in too deep, stability
of water, figments encircle the eye. this is
the buddy who took pound's chair at st. e's
who nursed lovers through the deathside of suicide
who taught verse to his cellmates at lorton

ah, but my fast walking buddy slowed down
jewel did this. she is a dancer & showed him
where the body ends. not at the flesh's tips
but with the shapes embossed in air when the form
flies away. jewel is a mother & taught him where
the body ends. not with images stranded in space
but at the core of her where new life curls & moves
jewel is a lover who took him where the body does not end

the great good love slowed my buddy down

THE CALL

this is what i fear
that the finder will come
for me & i will be nowhere
seen & she will call the name
i've never heard
& i will not answer
will never ride with her

she is never death

& the wall of hours parts
if the pose is true
i fear i will not pose true
& will remain

then the rift maker returns
voiceless. his footstep shakes
the moment i'm searching in

i remain. the blade
dulled by its labor
hums "never" carves "never"
on my place

the finder searches

i fear the finder
for i do not know her
the finder is not god
god is the hole
in knowledge

i fear never
never is the silent descent
of the sterile moment
i will not answer it

hope is the finder. i
am the lost

PEARL

—a secular love poem

if, as the yoruba say, all human beings
cover their nakedness with other human beings
how does friendship accomplish love? for i am
never so bare as i am with you. the best of you
abrades my edges away, smoothes & polishes our hours
together till i am free to lay my violations down before you
a maleficent track of hurts i have performed, secure
that you will not desert me there to walk that way again

you sketch for me the shapes & shadows of your fears
& i cradle those phantasms in a jocular fleece. you
lead me to those secret feminine alcoves we men
hear rumors of & i follow you, unconcerned that
my fragile manhood will dispel during the tour

remember those lessons in feminism you offered me
i thought myself a nimble student, noting everything
occasionally asking a probing question as a good scholar will
you recall applying jujitsu, throwing me down &
banging my head against the floor till i surrendered
ah pearl, how easily the conversation of friends
redacts yesterday. seen through you the way of men
is a dialectic of recoils between the hero & the thug
& the thug should die

last week we strolled next to time along the beach
trying to make the astrological signs—you honor
i dismiss—take shape in our sight. sidereal night
beneath an ocean sky that was articulate enough to read
the cosmic design all those antique shepherd eyes saw
named & assigned causality to. of course we never charted
them: there are too many turns among that many stars
& neither of us can drive an unfamiliar mile & not get lost

as the atlantic's waves turned 'round
at the tips of our toes you reminded me of burt lancaster's
line about the ocean in *atlantic city:* "you
should have seen it in the '50s; it was really something then"
well, we saw each other in the '60s; we were really
something then. consider that night in atlanta
at the after hours spot, the lincoln country club
when the middle-aged hustler tried to grind his way
to the other side of you on the dance floor &
you put a dunham arch into your spine so your hips
never touched. i thought, serves you right
for all those funkybutt poems you wrote about
slow dragging with block boys in dusky detroit basements
why, here's one now. he's just a little older

what else do we resemble? sometimes i think
your friend my wife & i must favor the weather
report with its simultaneous seasons. but us?
we're most like the syllogisms of barroom drunks
wise to each other but weird to the world

the thug in me puzzles in his atavism at the kind
of love this is that so eschews the physical
that wants no wet furtive groping in the dark
that nests in active peace through years of absence
& posts the last handwritten letters of this millennium

lovers & siblings do not have this. they have
too much to defend & defend against &
we do not. we have thoughts that match
& easy laughter. we have the wisdom of the ocean
& all the breeze that calls it there

PEARL 2

—Four Aperçus with Gnomic Appendices

I

pearl is frowning into her monitor
the squint of her eyes tells you she is worried
but it's her ear that's got her down
the pitch of her prose is flat. she's drawn
her people well enough: they have names
complexions, styles of dress, places to live
& go, but their voices are off-key; their lyrics
do not sing. they live against their background
& not inside it. pearl can't admit that the characters
she's made have tricked her so cunningly
they've conned her into a trap that she
cannot escape: the oblique state of almost-life
where her words glance off the real
but do not penetrate it. pearl knows
that she should walk away, just back out
of these people who refuse to inflame
no matter how hard she breathes on them
o shit! she sees it now. she's in the wrong person

in first person now pearl's bopping hard
she's typed so much her knuckles hurt &
her keyboard is blowing tunes

her people make a sort of rhythm section
under her in the way they improvise their lines
& moves: the ominous man stirs a tension
into the flow even when he's not in the room
the older woman keeps them on the one. eddie
when he enters, will be a tenor saxophone
the tessitura pearl prefers in her lovers
then ava will lean into the mike & croon
with him. their recitative will confect
into a ballad of delicate passion & staying close

writing is living strong in first person
in the revolutionary method of bebop
you make your phrases new
you swing hard through the changes
you break down the blues

2

pearl & zaron are sitting in a gazebo
forty steps from where high tide has moved
the beach. it's pouring down rain but there are holes
in the clouds that let streams of sunlight drizzle through
she is in loose beige diaphone; z is shoeless
& shirtless in a white linen suit that blackens
his mahogany skin. they have a jug of rum &
something between them. pearl is laughing hard, z
is conducting a story with his cigar. it is, of course
a lie, but a true one. as pearl remonstrates

with her balletic hands a slow wind blowing east
picks up their laughter & starts its
pelagic journey to the homeland shore

you can't write love if you don't have love
both parts of this truism are hard to pull off

3
pearl is in the kitchen. this is not where she lives
the lares & penates that guard her pantry
have few duties & must amuse themselves
with the creatures of imagination that she
& z emit. but there's this thing she does
with chicken breasts & mozzarella
that she's proud of & friends will be here soon
it's a housewoman moment she enjoys
for now but do not engrave this image
on your memory; pearl believes no butter
& batter can make women strong &
to commit to them would leave her issues
intact. she fears the universal sister mind
she wants to forge would etiolate
into invisibility if locked inside the home
no, she must take her causes to the page
where she can brew them & stew them
& serve them up to us

writing is wanting peace but knowing better

4

pearl & deignan are walking through the west end's
winter funk. it's a gray day but the breeze
is soft, the magnolias' fat leaves stubbornly green
deignan is in her last trimester. d in bloom
is more femme than ever & to her credit
she remains secure in her beauty, the grand camber
of her body now laminated in that lucent skin
that glitters fertile women. pearl is humming aretha
she has stocked advice for this moment
since she carried d & is now about to break it out
but in the way of the young d thinks herself
wise. no matter, pearl will lay it on her
anyway. they smile "i know more than you think"
smiles to each other, the signature countenance
of mother–daughter love, & it is cool
wisdom, after all, is more for broadcast
than for use

which is writing: music's other voice
hummed in the key of see. writing is where wisdom
goes to sing

THE TRUTH ABOUT KAREN

here in the solitude of distance
i see you clearer
you are carrying your mission
to the door, this time
it's stokely's last, painful year
you're saving by sculpting
a memory of fraternity
& revolution he can carry
into a champion's death in africa

now you are in your garden
amid herbs azaleas & shrubs
it is not a pristine patch
there are weeds among the blooms
i won't fatten the metaphor
of this snapshot: no aesthetic
of the imperfect or seeding
of blossoms in the urban etc.
it is enough that the theme
of your incessant busyness is
to find some funky thing
& make it better

even in sleep you are never still

beneath that woman
is the tender you
the one i breathe with
the passage to her opens
to the lightest touch
her transparency
in the nightlight breaks
on a soft blown kiss

i know that you *better* than you
she is far deeper
than her moans in the night
she is the love before birthing
the proof of the question, music
that makes the darkness live

my love, i am not a weak man
but i could not stand up
without your care. when
i'm in the bard's disgrace
with fortune & men's eyes
i call on the fool in you
who calls on the fool
in me & makes me whole

in the clarity of absence
i note that yours
is not a quiet beauty
it compels & has a radiance
we who love you stand inside of
& are home

THURSDAY, EARLY APRIL

at the top of the east a thin pink spray
behind a cloud infiltrates the dark
i think of you
i shave, go about my working day
my meetings are arid & won't resolve
i think of you
come home, walk our dog, observe
how timidly the tulips breach the ground
the new bird calls amid the festival of buds
in the maple trees that mark our block
& think, their songs are older south of here
where you are
i eat, hear the violations of the day
on *all things considered* & wish for you
shower, spread the lotion on my back
& wish for you. i go to bed with the radio
the sheets are cold on your side
nancy wilson sings *"i concentrate on you"*
i do
i read. the words won't hold together
perhaps tv? every corner of our house
makes ghost sounds. my sleep is thin
i dream

TOYIN'S SOUND

my first daughter
was home yesterday
she seems well
she's cut her hair
to a short bush
it helps you know
her eyes

she seems well
her music flows
ever easier. i thought
it perfect before
but now she's smoothed
her oboe's small angular
sound to the mature warmth
of aged granadilla
it's a chest tone now
it's double reed
a modal implant of the orient
in the ear of the west

her voice is in the making
of those reeds. hands
she's trained so carefully
to flutter keys

carve & scrape
the cane. she runs a scale
curses, whittles, runs
a scale & starts again
until the tone
is precisely her

curious, this way
of making music
unlike the piano
or saxophone or drum
or violin. it starts
with the way she shapes
the wind
        wrong
it starts with the way
she shapes the reed
that shapes the wind
until the oboe sings
in toyin's voice

soufflé light
in its richness
a depth
she'd be too shy
to offer you
in words

    * * *

back in chicago
the mozart adagio
for english horn arranged
for the same chamber
band that gil evans
spread out behind miles
on *sketches of spain*

this is toyin chanting
the evening poem
at winter's end
in the slow-blooming city
mozart has drawn this image
from that hidden cortex
at the center of solitude
where edgeless memory
composes
the soul's summation

the holy call it holy
for it is contented
to be eternal
toyin's rubato rhymes:
twilight music bridging
the lights
of the rufous sun &
the brilliant moon

her horn
is toyin's deep voice
singing through my silence
i inhale her sound: i
breathe it backwards
till the song sings me

ORIKI

—*for the birth of Kaji, twenty-five years late.*
After Kathleen Raine

into your ear i sing a name
& from that name there runs a line
& on that run ancestors chant
the elders dance, they build to you
from their mantra a rose exhales
a summer scent to cover you
within you there uncoils the line
woman to man to first-made child
to horizons beyond my sight
where settling light enwraps the cold
& in that light two hungry souls
combine combine to dream your name
& in their dream their love makes you
then from you there combusts a shout
around that shout there turns a ring
a stomp propounds a jubilee
in jubilee the ancients teach
a people rise, a people fall
we fall & rise & each new hand
will sculpt the shape of all the world
you have that force, it fires your smile
it fires your fury, fires the song
i sing to you. that you can *be*
is miracle enough for me

THE MEETING

hello. my name is ned &
i will be your facilitator
thank you for coming. we
are grateful for the distance
you have traveled & the thinking
you have brought
to this meeting. the restrooms
are to the right for men & to
the left for women

our topic today certainly
reverberates but before i say
that let me say we will be talking
in the following manner: i will talk
some of you will talk, i will record
facilitate & manipulate your
conclusions to my needs

which, i'm glad to say, are yours
but first, please introduce yourselves
to everyone by giving your name
affiliation, & the single, most salient
feature of your being. thank you

please keep all your remarks
brief. i will be very strict
about this. we have very little time
so don't repeat anything you've
heard or read. & now, let's hear
from you. but first i see
that my director is here

thank you ned. i'm grateful
for the distance you have come
we here value your values &
experiences. i won't take much
of your time because you don't have
much but i do want you to know
how much we value your thoughts
& the distance you have come
thank you. ned? thank you director

& now we're going to hear from
you. but first i want to prioritize
our conceptualizations during our
group face mail so we can
recontextualize them & calenderize
our interactive, proactive actualizations
on an ongoing basis, thereby repurposing
our core redundancies. but first

i see lunch is here

SONG OF THE LUDDITE

i am a quill & parchment
guy. machines that write
confound me, i don't use
"program" as a verb
or punch keys or anybody
else. i like being out of touch
& won't record your message
or have a phone in my car
this is the only page i'll answer

take me back to the 19th century
not the whole place, not the chattel
subjugation of my ancestors
or medicine without medicine
or the rape of the indian
or being stuck forever
where you were born. but give me

the romance of death
as a wonderfully enlightening
experience. the ideal of love
as an ocean we can backstroke in
i want to live
in a music whose melody
is liable for the state
of my soul

to travel slow enough to feel
the elements

i cannot value speed as much as the place
where i am. i want no instantaneous arrival
but let there be an amble in my journey

let them see me coming

& let them have me stay

RANDOM MEMORY

now, in this steel gray autumn
afternoon, small sun, small day
the *bolero,* all summer toned
no values but heat & color

pulses at my back. i do not love
the bathos but i'm grateful for any warmth
in this frigid moment. into this construction
intrudes a picture, an incongruent image

i have not seen in forty years
deep winter picture of a small brown
woman as old as memory. she paces
in the dark by a funeral hall window

it is night. she is a night tone
herself, indistinct before death
in death's season. all i see of her
is her mourning. it is wild & will

not be answered or consoled. this grief
extinguishes the rest of her. it burns
whatever love has left whatever flesh
speculation on who was lost

will not serve me here unless death's
method has meaning. was it willful?
a function of policy that redounds
to my people & so is mine to alter?

unless i am that woman, pacing &
weeping in the night, a small shade
among shadows. but that is just the flash
print of this undeveloped negative

i remember a perverse jealousy of her
for i had not yet loved enough to break
down at a loss; or i was glad
her eructating heart held enough fire

to so heat winter / so light night
or is it is proof of my life today that that
could be me weeping & being wept
over? of her? i do not worry

a heart so large has filled again

TIME WAS

time was liquor & weed made me love
the company of men. chest on the bar
man-talk of ballgames & easy women

story was all—story binds mellow men
to the bar. stories' bond is the high in the room
"she was so . . ." "so i hit him in . . ." " &
then she took . . ." the bar's light haze darkens

roll another one for my man. a snort
for her. the euphoria warms. high is a habitat

sober now i love the company of myself
but like all work this poem is a broken mirror
where am i inside it? concealed behind
the cracks in my face in that border of night
that never clarifies as dawn

harmony of the face reflected in the broken
glass singing of himself to himself. the smoke
the booze made chords of it, i hear them still
& wonder whether the solitude speaks truth to me

for who's lucid enough to be alone after hanging
out with the biota of hallucination? the dawn

i've told you never opens is not unpopulated
tho i can't attach names to what is found there
i knew the matter in it better then. could roll it
light it, chug it down, pass it to my friend, tell stories
through it "& then i said . . ." "we could have won if . . ."

i do not know that these moments are better
only that they are more peacefully recovered from

THE UNREQUITED
LUST BLUES

i went to sleep with you on my mind
don't know where you spend your nights
but i woke with you on my mind

o baby let me love you some time
if you don't it's gonna ruin my mind

when my thoughts are empty
they search for you

when my nights are empty
they swell with you

when my arms are empty
they enclose you

& i sleep with you
in my mind

ON HEARING GONZALO RUBALCABA AT BLUES ALLEY

Prelude

among the things i must have known
but have now forgotten is the skill of waiting
the room looks beaten, used, abused
as a good jazz club should. voices
unattached, waft away from the discipline
of words to feed my agitation
there is vague music on the sound
system. it does not help me. my seat hardens
i squirm, i wait, i write. art will be here soon

First Tune

gonzalo is at the piano. a small sturdy man
all in black in the muted haze. i think
he is shy & will not speak all evening
except to name his bass & drum
his first chords fold back into themselves, spare
& new, abjuring the metronome. he knows
we know his flash & wants us to learn his silence
brushes on the snare lift a drive

into the tune while gonzalo hangs out at the back
of the beat where prez & billie lived, rolls around
in every chamber of the beat, at home

Second Tune

i knew he would throw it. all those years
of czerny wrapped in salsa inside bebop
swing him beyond convention. swift families of notes
sprint by in hard rhythms. right hand
firing threes left hand crushing twos & fours
i spot a candle
through my neighbor's gin. its glow falls down
with the blues. bud powell knows you, gonzalo

Third Tune

meditation on the run

Fourth Tune

that's a sunny day. some restless djinn inside the crowd
cannot abide soft & slow. it sounds like opportunity
to them. the conversationalists confuse quietude
with vacancy & rush to fill this new reflection

rubalcaba values so. they drop their mutter
into the deep blue rests he has made for us
a vitiation of a moment as close to sacred as i know
the way to & i must now listen through their voices
to his invocation. (but the song! how much for the song?)
thoughts so tender they can only be sung. rhyme in the nursery
said at the bottom of my father's voice in the last sweet
instant before sleep. (*that* song: how much
for it?) long slow unpunctuated lines drift on the barest breath
(how much (the whispers break thru) for the goddamn song?)

        ah gonzalo, this is where we live
        making lines, building space, hoping
        the natter will leave our silence alone

ON HEARING SONNY ("NEWK") ROLLINS IN THE PARK ON A HOT SUMMER NIGHT

his worn hips barely support the horn
in his hands. it is gold & flashes under the fresnels

the sound is deep enough to live in. phrase turns to
brilliant phrase & the source never empties

i see in newk the hope of every limping
artist in the reluctant race against the slamming

of the lyric door when the senses atrophy
that dread day when a line of sound or verse

will hurt to render: the gripping eye
dims the active ear dims the trilling voice

dims. such fears we can contain in the long slowdrag
to humdrum death as long as the making works

there's newk in the picture of matisse who wields
a ten-foot brush as he lay in his deathbed

newk on the bus with count basie who
could only die on the road. see newk in ghana

with du bois as he started a fifteen-volume treatise
in his eighty-fifth year. so sonny blows the final plea

of the graying work maker—let me age anywhere
but in the horn

BOBBY'S BALLAD

bobby hutcherson is playing *polka dots*
and moonbeams & it's so clean & pretty
you'll miss the lyric if you listen lite. bobby
tests you to hear a voice on the other side of beauty
that asks then answers the questions
you never thought to pose. his vibes lift a soft
tintinnabulation to the ballroom's cornices
where the notes merge as bell tones do
then float back down upon us. if you could descry
bobby's song with your prismatic eye
it would describe a silver rain

i'm remembering bobby as i knew him
in 1964 on the lower east side
when nothing stopped anything we tried
we learned the discipline of freedom
& tuned our minds with the substance
of the hour—it could be weed, it could be
war, it could be instant, disposable love
it could be any of our little teeny revolutions

but now at the frisco bay his voice weighs
much more as i hope mine does. he's found
the balance that we fought to escape
& it's better than it was though the people

we used to be would laugh at us & call us
square. this is the failure of hipness
it stands casually in the mind of now
& pulls a reflecting shade down the eyes
so it can admire itself uninterrupted
carpe diem my ass: the now has no body
save what eidetic form reflection lays upon it

such is the truth of bobby's song
as he floats plump effulgent polka dots
into the argent beams of the bayside moon

NOTES ON A POEM: SUMMER (VERANO); CÉSAR VALLEJO

césar vallejo takes one look at summer
this lavishly berobed cleric who seeks
him out, & splits. it's a pointless call anyway
everyone has departed his, vallejo's
soul & all the jewels of july won't call
them back. but what's a sacerdotal season
to do if the soul it sought to wrap
into itself is vacant & will not be blessed?
compassionate césar has placed a rose
in autumn for summer's consecrated tears
to water. be careful says the poet
to the season, weeping upon the metaphors
of death might stir the graveyard stones
to life & then where are you? just trust
that autumn rose to live & die & live again
it always has / it always will

THE VIEW BEHIND

in the way of a searcher, a poet i like prowls 'round
inside his head trying to connect the paradoxes
the clumsy dance of is & ought to be, of form
& mortality, faithless future & desperate past
but these elements as we know them will not join
or we wouldn't have to wait for the instant of death
for clarity

all light refracts in there. he is startled
by his reflection, every time, & is not sure why
"i know the scent of this fell fellow," he says
of the inspired & bemused figment, "what
in st. augustine's wet dream is his name?" such hard
intestinal solipsism is a reduction of the fractal
soul whose subdivisions once parsed are endless
in their asymmetry: there is no atom or quark
of it that will not diminish to greater imperfection

which explains this blind stagger, this peculiar solo
dance of this angel on this pinhead floor. who else
but itself can the questing mind, poor unconquering thing
hope to encounter when it sets out to study its host

all his vision flows inward where smoke shadows cloud
the mutable passage between reason & being

each brilliant insight confounds the last
his mind a film noir darkly lit, the only spotlight
flares the eyes of the tender lover he imagined
into existence but debauched away with far too many
ideals. again & again he has limned the lucid apparition
he most desires into distortion. he cannot leave alone
these lego blocks of dust his inner circus
is constructed of & they blow apart
on a passing thought, leaving the fading soul
that held them whole to retreat even deeper
the lover, being him, cannot trust or be trusted
& he knows himself too well to reason with

THEOLOGY

sometimes the day
deceives me & i think
the ashes have settled
enough that i might
see two horizons
behind &
at last
know something
of reasons, any reasons
then the lost man
in me asks "why?"
& i am blind again

i try to digest
all i observe when
i search frantically
for god whose
most credible sightings
are within

it is the terror of "why?"
that god smoothly answers
without god why is
the cacophonous silence
that sets us screaming

but silence or scream
cannot call god
to be. the colors
of the earth
all that the senses feel
cannot call god
to be. "why?" cannot
call god to be
the oppressive distance
of the stars
the making, living
or losing of life
cannot call god to be

god must be the being
that calls itself
to be in the unspoken
quiet. i cannot hear
its voice amid the blazing
sirens that redden
the city's nights

i do hear those
who claim title
to god's inaudible song
their arias are brilliant
their voices swoop & trill
their meter
the body's own

they sing
our flesh's aversion
to decay and seek to carol
through the grave to merge
with some eternal chord

they claim never to doubt
a soul inhabits their
chest nor the widecast
of their prayer nor
the hearing of their god

they do doubt the wisdom
of their flesh, their earth
their reason. they do doubt
me for i am of this world
& revel in my skin

i walk in my skin in
my clothes in my streets
i see oppression
swirled in progression &
sometimes cannot divide them
i do marvel at the mysteries
& would contemplate them
forever if the press
of repairing those living
artifacts within my charge
would allow

do not allow me
to belittle the faith
of the godded
god, if god be
must claim faith
as its greatest gift
faith sees past vision
past reason, past birth
past our personal holes
in the fecund earth
but my faith is finite
does not turn corners
skim time or till
the cosmic soil
of the godded
my faith is local
& sustains by the hour

i would if i could name
what lives in me a soul
& in prayer commend it
to eternity. but to name
a soul is not to be eternal
to name that soul god
is not to be god

i crave all but live
on enough. atheist
i worship gesture

the play of the leaf
& the wind
the stand of the strong
against the wrong
it would satisfy
if my labor left
some small advance
some brief graffito
not even my name
to mark my living

let the next ones notice
that one herb-sized growth
touched by me
has shifted
toward the sun
if they must call it
god's work
from these lines
i will say no
it was mine

& they will say
even so

& i will answer
even so

OCTOBER

I

in the sullen shift to autumn
my city notes its mortality
& grows smaller. we file
our summer memories for the day
when the sun goes south for winter
one such must be this last moment
when the brilliant colors of ending
spread before the dingy tint of winter
with its day-long nights
& night-long blues
why this continual surprise
that all seasons & cities are transitional
as bright & as dull as this day
with its variable sky? think
of the clumsiness of bees confused
by their last, fatal mating. the summer
mist that collapses into frost
on the lawn. the single golden leaf
that floats in the rain-filled pothole

autumn will open & close as vague
as a man, with all the will to be
& the fear to become. it distorts itself
in the crooked light of an orange sun
that hangs on the lowest ledge of the west
all strange, all familiar, all fading away

2

the human form of autumn is a man
& a boy in a chevy with a sniper's porthole
in the trunk. they have hunted bus stops
& malls for lives to purge: sight shoot
drive away. they have an eye for the beloved
among us & deflate their flesh
with a single shot, deflate the living too
deflate the city with the sinking wonder
that misery conceives in the random circuit
of death. the hunters do not care. aim & click
the life goes out. woman, child, man
they do not care. black, asian, white
they do not care. a bullet costs less
than a side of fries; the hunt takes less time
than a shower. look & squeeze &
all the complex extensions of a life
reduce to food for the earth
they do not care. the man & boy of autumn
make winter. look & kill / see & slay

in the argument of seasons
we are sometimes sun sometimes wind
sometimes beginning sometimes end

9/11/01

for you don't count the dead / when god's on your side
— BOB DYLAN

with death no longer distant
we stand at the rubble of our always fragile
comity & are reminded of the unity of grief
& vengeance, this devastation that we turn
& turn again but cannot see the other side of

                                        walk me through it

quickly
dreams, for you know the lore our reason
will ignore of the malice that's milled
in the human will, the interminable them
& us of unctuous murder
with god on our side

                        that their innocents
must pay for our innocents

                     what king
has ever died of this? perhaps old
sere frederick barbarossa
who drowned in his armor
in the knee-deep waters of the iron river
on his way to sack jerusalem

                     the wise
chivalrous warrior dervish sala-al-din

99

never fought this war. he thought fell murder
to be christian work & would have sung
one hundred suras to burn away
the mephitic fog above the site
of this damnation

                our america
will refuse to sort the detritus
to find its own sin in it, but it lies there
smoldering, unexpiated by the flames
it's in the plain song of the new-made dead
who will chant it all the years that we live
we tilt the earth so the gold slides down
to us. we dress the starved illiterates
of the earth in the worst
of our culture & feign surprise
when they do not love us for it

                        & so i ask
the children's questions of this poem

                              what world
can be imagined where all the them & all
the us may cohabit in at least an assonant
peace? is all this inhumation truly about
the spelling of god's name? what tectonic force
can be ignited to pull the continents
of the human heart together in a time
when death is no longer distant?

THE CRUELEST MONTH

i think at last i am poet enough
to know the limitation of language
to say anew what has been said before
& again. which is why this late april
i will not compose the spring poem

eliot tried to uproot it
but it keeps growing back. spring is
after all more nettle than rose
the ejaculations of fornicating flora
attacking my sinuses, sarcophagus bugs
& exploding fungi in my soggy garden
chasing me back indoors

nobody sings of these
& what they do sing of is cliché
that spring is not winter
that there are more light-blasted hours
to admire the naive green
the april trees sun themselves in
that spring's warmth pares away
february's barrier clothes & exposes women
so nubile that at the sight of them
the years retreat from this out-of-season body
that winter told me would not last

ahhh spring

HOW FREEDOM WORKS
FOR SMALL THINGS

what do you do with the lark
that finds itself somehow
trapped in your living room
desperate & confused, in panic
at its first enclosure: wall
wall, glass that looks like liberation
but stuns the beak, & now
here comes you, the biggest mammal
it's ever been near. you think
well, this is a time
when sweet reason won't work
& terror is the only kindness

so you open a window
a stressed-out lark might like
the highest that you have
get a big broom & threaten
the poor bird, chase it up & up
till it finds the hole in hell
you've made for it &, free
at last, flees your happy home

hating you

VILLANELLE FOR THE HELL OF IT

i lose myself in odd familiar places
i speak aloud to no one on the street
of dream issues, to dream faces

when detected i pretend a song. grace
is dear. it is my singing self i meet
lost alone in this odd familiar place

which of me wanders? which holds to some trace
of the real? with what wisdom do they speak
its dream language, face to fading face?

it is the freedom that my dream portrays
i seek. cold reason's nourishment's less sweet
than singing in this odd, familiar place

my dream friends are true. in formless space
mutable, vague yet never incomplete
they walk with me in these odd comforting spaces

the self i lose, the self i find replaces
my song the beacon, whose comforting heat
restores my lost self to familiar places
singing dream lyrics to retreating faces

THINGS I MISS FROM MY YOUTH

1. Shooting Stars

night
made a luminous
& speckled hood
over my southern town
the milky way
was solid white
gods of all lands
could ride across it

you stitched together
your own
constellations
& they were the gods
who rode

every night thin
white streaks etched
the velvet black
you & your friend
watched for them
but they seemed

to fall in
only one eye
          decorating
those perfect hours
before sleep

now i must travel
great distances to find
a textured sky. now

light broadcasts up
from the city
          now night
depopulates
the heavens

now
only the great
round moon
bears fantasy

2. A Hometown I Could Walk Across

it took
about an hour
at a pace that
allowed the notice
of birds & victory

gardens &

        "how do's?" to

the old folks swinging

on their porches

i knew them all

by face, most

by name

they called me

after my father

little alfred

the houses all looked

right according to what

i knew: the fine ones

by the river

where the gentry

lived, the shotgun

flats where most black

folks lived

the two-box frame

ones in between

even the empty ragged

houses that sagged

into ruin

& melded

with the weeds
looked right
i knew time &
the fat brown
earth
would consume them

i did fear
the tall grass
where rattlers
& copperheads
might live

i now walk
in the city &
i still fear
the high grass

3. Hummingbirds

dying
my mother complained
the little yellow
bird she liked
so much
never came by
her window
any more

she tried
to remember its song
& hated
to think it
might be gone
its color
went so well with
the hot green outfit
my hometown sported

i miss hummingbirds
more. they
have no song
no color no
shape & a funny
long beak

i remember their
movement & think
of modern dancers'
astonishing darts
to unexpected
places, startling
as shooting stars

hummingbirds love
to hang still
in space

with their beaks
in bright flowers

give them a song
& what kid
wouldn't want
to be a hummingbird

4. Aunt Julia's Mushy Fried Mullet

she stuffed her
house with the paper
flowers she made
screaming things
so loud

you thought you
smelled them—too
sweet for nature
it was her
perfume you smelled
it weighed a ton

her trade bought
every flower

mother said
sis julia
was a fast young
thing. i do know

she married
six men &
divorced none. this
caused her much stress
when social security
got computers

true: aunt julia died
went to heaven &
returned with news of
the celestial chorus
& which kin
soloed in it, etc.
the bastards laughed
at her

aunt julia
couldn't cook
a lick, but i loved supper
with her. why
didn't hummingbirds
hang 'round her? she
had the color
of her flowers &
the sweetness
of her perfume

too rich to find
in the world

5. *Pay Envelopes*

little sacks
of cash they put
in your hand
at six o'clock on
saturday

insufficient
by miles
but tangible
not metaphysical
like today's invisible
wages with
less body
than aunt julia's
holy ghost
whose mass she
almost could
calibrate

i miss
silver dollars &
fifty cent
pieces. big
rocks of money
you tied up
in a kerchief or

a sock
the sock knot
could make
a weapon

in a schoolyard
fight with the bully
big six
oodiboy used
it so: a sort of
money bludgeon

i guess oodiboy's
doing well now

THINGS I DON'T MISS FROM MY YOUTH

1. My Schoolbooks

often the covers
were loose
the inside front
was a directory
of the white school
across town

debbiejean &
skipper hall & tippie
tommy & terry
tebbetts. their
scribbles in
the margins
their doodles by
the headings

they had fingered
all the learning
before the books came
to us. our knowledge
was handmedown

used, discarded

2. Peeing Behind the Trashcan in the Alley
Next to the Bookstore

it wasn't just
that the signs
regulated
what you ingested
where you voided

white fountains colored
fountains; white
toilets
colored toilets

& it wasn't just that
their nice word
for us was colored
making us into
something someone
had taken
a crayon to
it was
that they defined
our limits down
to our viscera
downtown
was theirs & we
could not carry

our effluents
to it
      my only passage
from this verdant wasteland
was books & other vagrant
art: opera from the met
on saturdays. bebop
from jazzbo's purple
grotto on clear nights
                              its sound starlight thin
from the stretching
of its wavelength

i walked
most often to
the one bookstore
six blocks from relief

& after a poor snack of
the caldwells, maughams &
spillanes
out to the rat's
shelter in the alley
to solve
my bladder's urgent
imagination

3. Not Knowing Better

florene barco moved
to philadelphia &
on a visit home told
us she went
to school with
white kids

it was a lunar image

everything shouted
inferior
to us
        the patterns
we walked. the ease
with which they
commanded. that
we could not live

by the river
word of lynching
farther south & of course
the signs. i
thought it all to be
as much of nature
as the night sky
the birds of the air

the notion of place
meant not where
you stood but how
you talked
to a white man

place was
the wet brown earth
your knees
sank down in

& philadelphia
was the crescent
moon

4. *Aunt Bud's '30 Something Chevy*

ugly little black coupe
she wouldn't get rid
of though aunt bud
was the only one
in the family
with money

uptight woman, she
drove it through homes
taking something of the life
she found there
she thought some

poor, blacker
than her, families
bad & carted
their kids to church
at ten cents a head when
gas cost a nickel

she collected clothes
for poor folks
in the country, gave
them out at hog
killing time &
brought home hocks
& hams, offering
us the chitterlings
but we hated chitterlings
they stank
the house for days

aunt bud took
in kids from her baddest
families & worked
them toward salvation
for five cents an hour
                          she taught
waste not
& made them eat
their ice cubes

a few years
with aunt bud &
the boys became
winos & the girls
whores & that chevy
took her to
more lives to empty

we'd call it
a classic today

REDEMPTION SONG

These songs of freedom / they're all we ever had

—BOB MARLEY

they say vuyisile mini, whose name's
a lyric, pinioned & wan, went
to the noose with a smile on his lips
& assault in his eyes. they hung him
for a song but they couldn't hang the song
zulu sotho tswana xhosa sang it
in impeccable thousand-voice choirs
"look out verwoerd / black people
gonna get you" in four-part harmony
on the train to the city
at the lorry stops, the markets
in the kitchens of the boers. "look
out verwoerd" in the mines, bass
choirs in robben island prison
everyone's voice knew where to go
& it felt like joy
"we're coming for you"

they danced the toyi-toyi to it
on the marches, dance that lifts
the shoulders till the body follows
then the knee-cracking stomp

& it felt like joy. on your face verwoerd
"black people gonna get you" through
the picture-postcard valley whose hills
multiplied the chord they skipped
the shebeen steps of the phatha phatha
before they turned to face the guns
"look out. beware." even when their song told
of the death of a hero it felt like joy

when the boers had torn the spirit
of soweto & time itself seemed
made of mud the children stood & sang
"no, we'll not be taught in afrikaans"

& after the revolution in song, after
the ululated lyric had freed mandela
to dance his way to the balcony above the millions
there were not streets enough or hills enough
to hold all the song

& when they opened the pauper's grave
to retrieve vuyisile's bones they sang
no threnody at all but clicked the song
a smile creates on its way to the noose
"look out, look out" in the skeletal
tenor the wind blew in seamless sound
through the bone-toned flute
& if felt like joy

THE FIRST SEVENTY

in the '30s the child i was
did not doubt the wisdom & wonders
of the world or my place in it
i lived in my head
& spent my life in contemplation of wind
"rosa belle" sis minnie told mother
"a.b.'s been standing in front
of my house for an hour, looking up
in the air. i stood by him & looked
up too, but the sky was empty
no birds no planes no clouds
now he's got the whole street
staring up at nothing"
broke as we were nobody told me
there was a depression on
i learned to read & had less need
of clouds

in the '40s i had three years in the bosom
of holy mother the church & the baltimore
catechism & learned to find mortal sin
in every intuition. i toted the host
in cassock & surplice & fought
my hormones' terrible invasion
of my piousness, swung the thurible
with too much vigor as i peeped

across the censed altar at seraphic
dolores stubbs, two years older
with cherokee hair & skin the patina
of lucid midnight, on her knees
telling her beads, not dreaming
of me at all, lust-lost in my latin &
thinking the devil's thoughts with such rapture
i had to turn atheist to save my soul

my view of wwii refracted
through the convexity of comic books
& movies, had me seeing duke wayne
& all the caped heroes bashing nazis &
other malefactors into cross-eyed stupor
it would take me half a life to wonder
why captain america never visited
my neighborhood where our local fascists
ruled in christian righteousness
the narrative of the times was sketched
without my image except as a priapic
chicken-thieving paragon of bestial dumbness
barely fit for the back of a plow

well, stepin fetchit, snowflake
willie best, mantan moreland, butterfly
mcqueen stole every scene they entered
so give them that. give them the flair
to shine the black light with such wattage
it blurred the stars. concede to them
the grace to win when cast as lost

bebop saved the '40s. a clear wind
blew jazzbo collins into my home
from his nest in the "purple grotto" deep
in the core of the apple & in walked bud
with bird & diz & fats & monk & max
& all the cats. the sounds were faint
on my philco. i had to press my ear
against the music to assemble those cycles
of fifths, flatted to the devil's interval
those fractured chords, vertiginous changes
& bent arpeggios that swiveled around
in my head & shaped new consciousness

bebop was news that my people were moving

you can't scat bop & bow to a redneck

i got laid in the summer of '52 & went off
to howard where roi taught me cool. this was
mccarthy's d.c., jim crowed & tinted
a monumental beige, devoid of the shimmer
of art save buck & his band at abart's

howard held the moot for *brown v. board*
& hearing thurgood's homeboy gravamen
lifted my nascent wisdom to the height of a man
these off-years taught me that we do walk
in the ineluctable ballistic of history
whose force will raise the worthy

in such times a people make their angels
& there at the pivot was rosa parks, beautiful
fine-boned, who rested her aching feet &
sat down on the bus that changed the route
of the world

my first were night poems: of a tree
that embosomed the moon & the fool
in repose beneath her. of wandering wet
deserted streets, staring at dark windows
wondering if these people also die. white
my mad painter friend, tried to change his style
to abstraction but found the surreal instead
if you turned his pictures upside down
the beasts of the id flew out, hunting the source
of your tranquility in edacious landscapes
just beyond your dreams' ephemeral borders
everyone could see them but white

i got laid again

in '57 i moved to n.y. & caught monk's return
from brutal exile to the five-spot. trane joined him
on the stand with double-stopping wilbur ware
no music has ever so joyously inured to itself
such explosively advancing revelation, note to
phrase, tune to set, night to ignited dawn. the ineffable
message those instruments sang to me—not the learning
we parse from text, but the meaning we feel lost & blind

for the lack of. hard & softly blown, full lives compressed
in the blazing instant of the horn
in such moments i understood the fear of art
it's in the sudden departure to places i'd never heard of
when all i came for was a little froufrou
to tack onto the dimly lit walls of my consciousness
i did not hear this music so much as it occupied me
pulled me up, eyes closed to the sonic light
brain thrown hard against the back of my skull
in the sharp upward acceleration at more gees
than i could handle. my suffering silent reason yelled
stop! this air fires blue hot! there's danger in this flight
but instead my mouth gaped in a numinous yes
in the smoky dark, screamed yes monk yes trane yes yes yes

how it happened? imagine john coltrane starting the gig
enclosed in a crystal egg & thelonius dancing
the monk dance around him & trane stammering
his opening lines, a halting brilliance that did not flow
& monk dancing the invocation of swing dance
till the line coalesced with the geometric burn
the broken sword architecture of lightning
shattered the egg in a storm of jewels
& out stepped john, wailing, this godzilla
tenor player who took me out & out & out
for the next ten years. i have heard gould play bach
seen cunningham & fonteyn dance; known
the primal strokes of van gogh & pollock; read
the verse of the masters & all, all have remade me

but no art has so blown my inner spaces clean
so propelled me through the stages of being
as john coltrane live. i tried not to miss a note

i often think of the '6os in mystic terms
the sweet reflective plucking of lotus leaves
in search of the jewel in the obscure heart of me
in truth it was the opposite: a desperate sprint
down the long corrupted alley to the outer self
possessing a young man's definitive clarity
i wanted revolution in america. i could see
myself in that photograph of fidel & che
in guerilla camouflage, riding into havana
on a handsome horse, smoking a fat cigar

i studied the twin mahatmas, martin &
malcolm. the south marched to
the mellifluous martin, who saw equality
as a moral state. in n.y. i heard malcolm
el haji red, for whom revolution was an act
of manhood. community was the word
of power. it extracted my jewel & appraised
its value against the notion of home
which i no longer could locate with certainty
malcolm asked me, how can you garden beauty
in your weed-infused ether when your people
are firing the streets in the quest for justice?
was home the society of artists, my first cohort
of the mind? was home those depressed acres

where my race had been herded, the inescapable ghetto
of no hope with a hammer? was home the romance
of africa whose kings' legends were as grand
as arthur & charlemagne? i had a son to this
conflict, named him malcolm, & wronged him
more than i have ever wronged with my choice

i chose a home in that world of interdigitating
genes of brown memory that bound us, less by
the deathstench of the middle passage than by
the songs we made in field & factory to get us through
my choice of commitment was karen &
the southern struggle. her tribe was sncc
& if they owned fear they burned it for fuel
alabama, mississippi—hear the cadence
of those names. they drum the accents of murder
in the swamp, of hooded nightriding baby
blasters. the sncc folk brought a courage to the backwoods
that my father's age would have recognized as madness

karen & i made toyin, whose music i have told
you of, & kaji, whose poem i have not yet written
in the schizophrenic '70s as we watched our movement
fade. the *colored in the rear* signs were down &
the targets misted opaque. marvin gaye emigrated
from *"what's going on"* to *"let's get it on"*
i hid in the poolroom from the bougies
learned to play one-pocket from junebug
& bank from lagrange shorty. elmo

said my eye was so good i could see a hair
on a gnat's ass but he beat me for forty dollars that day

my hair unbraided was six inches tall & my clothes
were illustrated. ah quiana. your flowers are faded now
your forests defoliated, their pacific fauna stripped
of their lovely orange fur. but the power rules
in blue & gray & would tolerate no flair & so the '80s
never came. the wealthy bought them wholesale
remember the slogans: the revenge of living well?
let them eat ketchup? he who dies with the most toys
wins? remember art as corruption? benign neglect?
an empty man with a vamp's smile ruled us
& we earned him, for our offerings were lame &
our struggle slack. even music lost its heartbeat

my life distilled into the amniotic succor
of mundane love: the electrical affection of a wife
who learned commitment in dangerous struggle
the option of my son's screenplay
the lachrymose aesthetic of sonatas well played
by my teenaged daughters

my work was paper & procedure, two walls
from making art & i learned the process
of compromise that auden tells us
aging is. i wrote no poems for twenty years

here, at the end of centuries, at the millennium's close
i am running from the chiliasts who stalk the antichrist
in verse & painted line. i will make no more children
but i have my poems back. they tell me to accept
that I am another lingering man, alive in the subjunctive
obedient to the law of the crossroad of time flesh
& spirit, the codes of the tensions & releases of art
& history, the mutable landscape of trails made & litter left
surely some of this must be gift: perhaps some might be
monument as well. tell my gravestone when you see it

i do question the nature of a nature
that directs the young to courses that veer
so far from the ones that we charted for them
how their dance & music elude us as bebop eluded
my father. how they rap too damn fast for an ear
trained on eckstine to follow. their reticulated rhythms
rock the web where i venture tremulously. their artists
sample our work in the conceit that nothing can be new
so the old must be cut in new patterns

as if we made it all

as if we made it well

WRONG AGAIN

help me with this: a laconic bodhisattva
i'm headed out into what feels like summer
on the sun in a quietist kind of mood
looking to elevate to a hipper state
less cluttered by the bric-a-brac
that fills the pockets of my soul
but where to do this? this is d.c.
& the mall's full of tourists &
the park's too dangerous to sit lotus
(not that i can fold like buddha
the leg tuck would break my knees)
home won't work; it's too full of me
& the dog will want walking. but who says
you gotta sit to levitate? i've got the buddha
belly so i've just gotta flush my mind
right? use the cosmic force of nothing
to blow it out so all the luminosity of the void
has room to enter, lighter than helium, & lift
me by the cortex. i imagine the sound of silk
stroking a gong, imagine insight without words
or pictures. i will smile mysteriously
with the lucent clarity of knowledge
i've always had but been too daft

to know i knew. the moments of birth
& death must be lit this way, wonder
too complete to notice matter

but you gotta be somewhere to be
nowhere & there's the heat & the tourists
the arthritic knees & the house of me
so i turn three times, bow to the void
proclaim myself a rhinestone in the hall of light
go back indoors & order triple gelato

ORIGINS

eve rose first
saw her skin
matched the claret
mud of the riverbank
thought "i am
the first of firsts"
stepped out
to touch the day

        tall among the wildebeest
        & the placid lion
        in the one-month shade
        of the baobab
        adam stood
        observed the mating race
        of the cheetah
        the cruel pattern
        of zebra on zebra
        the wine-skinned eve
        & felt his blood

in the conversation
between innocence &
nescience
eve & adam considered

the notion
of life: this food
this body, mammalian
birth at the baobab
root, what to do
in sunlight
what to do
in darkness

days tumbled out
of days; the quiet waters
of night eroded
the moon's mutant
shapes. one by one
eve & adam named
the elements
of their neighborhood
but could make no word
for their greatest find
this magnetic elevation
above a world
already new

what do the newborn see
when they have never seen?
knowing nothing
they knew more
their virgin news

found on their knees
in the mating fold
of lion cheetah zebra
by remnants
of light / blinking forms
of shadow in the tepid breeze
beneath the baobab

        what the mind conceals
        the heart reveals
        love lust friendship
        trust, indistinct
in a nation of two

IN WHICH I SLAM THE WILSON

in relief of the cluttered excess
that futile ambition & imagination
conspire to make i ease into reverie

there the youthful genius me
flexible & strong & a marvel to behold
blocks a jam of kobe's & sprints the floor
to rise well over shaq, high as the heavy air
will buoy, & slam the wilson home

i do this in a transcendent state
more of nirvana than of grace. they marvel
not that i care, that i am unaffected
by my gifts. tired but calm i say "no"
to the press. "i am more artist
than athlete. a single season in the nba
was enough. i leave it now to make clean
energy, complete my sixth symphony
work on my left hand or i will never reach
art tatum's standard. the critics
might be satisfied but i am not"

DEATH POEM

we in our frailty paint death
in black unspeaking mystery
the inexorable terrible wonder

we run in mark-time terror
to escape. the dead
must know that life is more

the question; death the answer
the living cannot learn. i would
ask them what the living know

of life? that life is made of love
itself insensitive to definition
too easy to say, too difficult

to mean, too hard to sort
the truth of when need is
the breath of its saying

yet our most frail & vital
aspect rides love to love's
belly where it swells & swells

seed to root, bud to fruit
the swinging heartbeat's 4/4 syncopation
in the glorious arch of the womb

we know the living heart may
not sequester from the newly
born that fragile center

that reason reserves from lovers
for the reconstruction it must do
after those vile rendings

when passion deliquesces into tears. o
but the life we build together flourishes
apart from us, a greater making

than art or news. we can shout yes
to it in its distant mirror
or dance with it squeezed to our chest

as the heart's polyrhythms drive
the silent melody the living harmonize
when they do / if they do

we know birth itself is a greater
question. this death of death is a gift
to whom? i think to the makers

who empty & fill in the cause
of renewal, who flow to the form
who inflame to the new. but how true

a gift is life to the newly born
when the only love we can pledge
is our own? all we can give is hope

that this new heart will find a heart
to ride. that it builds itself in the world
& is not built by the world

that it loves & is loved

2

& what do the living know
of death? we confuse death
in the mirror with our failings

of the hour: how we do not shine
always but sometimes dim the light
but death shines too. it is not true

to its symbols, for death is made
of bright memory. death's craft
is absence, immediate & binding

we see death as that spectral house
we must never enter that awaits
us at the turn of every corner

we fear that its chambers will be
empty & the vacant loves that once
sustained us will not receive

us there. but death is naked
of all form & does not inhabit
darkness. those few life travelers

who have peeked inside its open door
tell of a calling sun of a light
that signs the simple question

was it worth it? all those sprints
& stalls, did they make even a wind a
breeze a breath? asks with a nodding peace

that is the smile 'round nothing
of the sitting buddha's still-shut eyes
it is not death who throws terror

at every aspect of our living
the awe of its ubiquity so great
we build whole gods to dispel it

no, that is the work of the living
as the dead say only silence
in their knowing glow

CONCLUSION

If I knew the way from here I would leave this placid place & return to the tropic estates of desire where mystery directs the moment & the past is lost to the blindfold dive into what comes next. I would replace understanding with passion, for the state of serenity empties fast & those who populate it do diminish for all their unity of thought.

Irenic illusion supports the fraud of sanity as the heavy years descend if only because I have learned enough to name most parts of my nature, even the extraneous ones that have fallen away one by one, & such solipsism must pass for accomplishment. But who can argue that a man who cares more for solutions than for causes is made of the same good stuff as fertile youth?

So makes a man a man of the elements of time. Restrained by wisdom & thus less wise in my forfeit of impetuosity, I hope I can reclaim this force at will; after all, I reflect, I threw nothing away, only gave a home to dissipation as it settled into me. I reassure myself with the belief that commitment lives in there too, honing its sword & shouting instructive aphorisms into the inner ear. But how articulate *is* this quietude that has stationed itself at such telescopic distance to chart the movement of things & beings? What does it really see from so remote an aerie? Tints & forms? Surely it cannot see what it used to feel when it put its hand upon every need it came upon. More important, who does silence tell what it has learned, if silence is capable of learning at all?

Lust at least was aggressive in its innovations. One could trust the truth of lust if not its jagged works, but this cool passive diffidence aspires only to defend its place, at best to make a garden there. Attract some butterflies. Build an appropriate wall.

It never earns a song; no song is ever called for it.

NOTES

Ambiguity is an honored device in poetry, but confusion over archaic slang or references that are not explained by context, do not help the poem. Therefore, I have supplied the following notes.

After Vallejo: "Orisha" are demigods of the Yoruba religion. "Congueros" play conga drums, "bongoseros" play bongos, "timbaleros" play timbales. "The mother of waters" refers to Yemajo, an important Orisha who is often equated with the Virgin Mary. "The saint at crossroads" is the erstwhile St. Christopher, equated with Elegua, whose name is invoked in the beginning and ends of Santeria ceremonies.

Dear John Coltrane: I didn't realize it until I'd been through several drafts, but I must have had at least the title of Michael Harper's fine poem in my head when I wrote this. As the title integrates with the body of the poem I could find no way to change it.

Why Do They Call It Nightmare . . . : A "jiva" is one of the Hindu names for the spirit.

Groovin' Low: The title is a play on a bebop tune of Dizzy Gillespie's entitled "Groovin' High." Whatever Diz was blowing about, this poem concerns aging. "paradiddles, ratamacues, & flams" are technical terms of drumming.

Ghost: The eminent theologian Elaine Pagel wrote an excellent book entitled *The Origins Of Satan,* in which she described how Satan's image changes according to the politics and state of a people at any given time. I read it, thinking that there'd be a few poems in it. The chapters yielded none, but the preface told how she'd come to study the subject of angels after her husband died in a hiking accident, and how he remained such a tangible presence in her life. This poem issues from that preface.

Hellfighters on Parade: This band had a huge impact in France, and laid the foundation of the large expatriate community of African American musicians, artists, and intellectuals that became the under-discussed phenomenon that was known as Paris Noir. You can see actual footage of this parade, with Bill Robinson's drum major strutting spliced in, in the film, *Stormy Weather.*

Metrarie: "houngan & mambo" are priest and priestess of the Vodun religion. "Calinda" and "congo pile" were African-derived dances that were prominent in Lousiana in this period. The "loa" are Vodun demigods. "Papa Legba," "Baron Samedi," and "Damballa" are loas. The "guede" are lesser, mischievous creatures—think elves, but not really.

When Black People Are: "Orangeburg" refers to the city where South Carolina State College is located. This is only one of the historically Black colleges where, during the 1960s, students experienced the same kind of murderous assault that took place at Kent State, but you never hear of those incidents. All of the people named in this poem were civil rights activists, with the exception of CBS anchorman Walter Cronkite.

Another Love Song: An "upas" tree is a Southeast Asian evergreen with a poisonous breadfruit-like yield. It is said to drip deadly poison on anyone who lies beneath it, or who even comes near it. It has also become a synonym for a poisonous influence, or institution.

The City Poet on the Stroll: This poem covers a fifty-year span, and uses dated vernacular terms. "The roller" is 1950s slang for the police, particularly those in cars. "Jelly Roll" is the seminal New Orleans pianist Jelly Roll Morton. Morton spent some of his last years in Washington. "Duke," of course, is Duke Ellington, who was born there. "Cab's neat seats with reet pleats" is an expression that the great swing bandleader Cab Calloway used to describe his zoot suit pants. Yardbird is Charlie Parker; the beboppers gave ivy league attire a different kind of cool. "Pegleg Bates at the Howard" refers to the one-legged tap dancer in a show at the Howard Theatre, in the 1950s still a major tour stop for black entertainers. Don't laugh; Pegleg could do it. "The Stroll" is the streets. "Dooji" and "scag" are old terms for heroin. "Pound's chair at st. e's" refers to St. Elizabeth Hospital for mental patients. It's where Ezra Pound was interned following WWII.

The Truth about Karen: The first stanza concerns a celebratory event that my wife, Karen, mounted for Stokely Carmichael / Kwame Ture during the last months of his life. It brought together most of the leadership and many of the troops of the civil rights movement.

Toyin's Sound: "Granadilla" is a tree, fast disappearing, whose wood is used to make oboes & clarinets. The reference to the Mozart Adagio for English Horn concerns an arrangement that was done for Toyin Spellman and members of the Chicago Civic Orchestra.

Oriki: Among the Yoruba, the first sound a newborn child hears is an elder singing its private name to it, along with the legend of its lineage. The form is an old Scots one in which each line extends an image from the one that precedes it. There is a reference to the ring shout, an African retention that still survives in the South today, at least in a folkloric context.

Redemption Song: "Zulu sotha tswana xhosa": all South African tribes. "Shebeens" are bars in the townships. "Patha patha" is a dance step. "Soweto" is a large township in Johannesburg.

The First Seventy: Jazzbo Collins was a d.j. in New York who played modern jazz. He claimed to be broadcasting from "the purple grotto," the kind of fantasy world that bebop hipsters loved to create. "roi taught me cool" refers to LeRoi Jones, as Amiri Baraka was then known; he was my intellectual guide for many years. "White / my mad painter friend" is William White, a gifted painter who never cracked the gallery scene during his too brief life. "double-stopping wilbur ware" speaks of the innovative bassist out of Chicago who played with Thelonius Monk during these years. He used a lot of double-stops, i.e., plucking two strings at once during a melodic solo passage. "Her tribe was sncc." I probably don't need to explain this, but many younger (than middle-aged) readers might not have heard of the Student Non-Violent Coordinating Committee, the most radical of the Southern civil rights organizations. If you don't know them, they are well worth reading up on. "ear trained on eckstine," refers to the great modern jazz crooner, Billy Eckstine.

A.B. Spellman is both a founding member of the Black Arts Movement and one of the fathers of modern jazz criticism. Before moving to Washington, DC to begin his thirty-year tenure at the National Endowment for the Arts, Spellman was an active poet, radio programmer, and essayist in New York, the poet-in-residence at the Morehouse College in Atlanta, and a visiting lecturer at Emory, Rutgers, and Harvard universities. He has also been a regular jazz commentator for National Public Radio and has published numerous books and articles on the arts, including *The Beautiful Days*, a chapbook of poems first published in 1965, and *Four Lives in the Bebop Business*, a classic in the field of jazz criticism that is now available as *Four Jazz Lives* (University of Michigan Press).

Between 1975 and 2005, Spellman worked at the National Endowment for the Arts, first as the Director of the Expansion Arts Program and, for the last decade of his term, as Deputy Chairman. In recognition of Spellman's commitment and service to jazz, the NEA created the A.B. Spellman NEA Jazz Masters Award for Jazz Advocacy. Additionally, the Jazz Journalists Association voted to honor Mr. Spellman with its "A Team" award, and he received the Benny Golson Award from his alma mater, Howard University, for his service to jazz. *Things I Must Have Known* is his first full-length collection of poetry.

COLOPHON

Things I Must Have Known was designed at Coffee House Press, in the historic warehouse district of downtown Minneapolis. Fonts include Caslon and Aberration.

FUNDER ACKNOWLEDGMENTS

Coffee House Press is an independent nonprofit literary publisher. Our books are made possible through the generous support of grants and gifts from many foundations, corporate giving programs, state and federal support, and through donations from individuals who believe in the transformational power of literature. Publication of this book was made possible, in part, through special project support from the National Endowment for the Arts. Coffee House Press receives general operating support from the Minnesota State Arts Board, through an appropriation by the Minnesota State Legislature and from the National Endowment for the Arts, and major general operating support from the McKnight Foundation, and from Target. Coffee House also receives support from: an anonymous donor; the Elmer and Eleanor Andersen Foundation; the Buuck Family Foundation; the Patrick and Aimee Butler Family Foundation; Stephen and Isabel Keating; Mary McDermid; Tom Rosen; Stu Wilson and Melissa Barker; the Lenfesty Family Foundation; Rebecca Rand; the law firm of Schwegman, Lundberg, and Woessner P.A.; the James R. Thorpe Foundation; the Woessner Freeman Family Foundation; the Wood-Rill Foundation; and many other generous individual donors.

To you and our many readers across the country, we send our thanks for your continuing support.

Good books are brewing at coffeehousepress.org

Printed in the USA
CPSIA information can be obtained
at www.ICGtesting.com
LVHW041213210924
791747LV00002B/152